100 Prayers
God Loves to Hear
100 Praise Songs

created by Stephen Elkins

Illustrated by Tim O'Connor

A Division of Thomas Nelson Publishers

NASHVILLE   DALLAS   MEXICO CITY   RIO DE JANEIRO

Library of Congress Control Number:

Elkins, Stephen.
  100 prayers, 100 praise songs / created by Stephen Elkins ;
illustrated by Tim O'Connor.
     p. cm.
  ISBN 978-1-4003-1549-9 (padded hardcover)
  1. Children—Prayers and devotions. 2. Contemporary Christian music—Juvenile literature. I. O'Connor, Tim, ill. II. Title. III. Title: One hundred prayers, one hundred praise songs.
  BV265.E45 2010
  264'.23—dc22

                    2010010351

mfr: R.R. Donnelley/Shenzhen, China/July, 2010—PO# 106899

10 Bible Verses about Prayer

*Smile, **pray**, and be thankful. This is how God wants you to live.*
—from 1 Thessalonians 5:16–18

*When you **pray** for the things that Jesus wants for you, He will give them to you.*
—from John 14:13–14

*Be happy because Jesus loves you. When you have troubles, **pray**.*
Then wait for God to answer you.
—from Romans 12:12

Sometimes it is hard to do the right thing, even when you want to.
***Pray** to God, and He will help you do what is right.*
—from Matthew 26:41

***Pray** in the morning. **Pray** in the night and all the day in between.*
***Pray** about big things and little things. **Pray** about everything!*
—from Ephesians 6:18

*Don't worry. **Pray** to God for what you need. Then thank Him for all that He gives you.*
—from Philippians 4:6

*God wants to hear what you have to say. He will always listen when you **pray**.*
—from 1 John 5:14–15

*When you don't know what to **pray**, the Holy Spirit will **pray** for you.*
—from Romans 8:26

Everyone makes mistakes. When you mess up, say "I'm sorry,"
*and then **pray** to God, who will forgive you.*
—from James 5:16

*Don't **pray** just so that other people can see you **pray**. **Pray** when no one can see you.*
God will see you. He will hear you and answer your prayers.
—from Matthew 6:5–8

Table of Contents

A child's Grace

The psalmist once wrote, "There is none like you, O Lord" (Psalm 86:8). That's because God alone is great and mighty. Everything you see around you can be traced back to His mighty hand. Your clothes, your home, even your food is all given by God!

God is great, and God is good,
And we thank Him for our food.
By His hand we all are fed,
Give us, Lord, our daily bread.
—Traditional

Take time each day to say "thank You!" to the One who gives you all good things. God is truly *great*!

MY LITTLE PRAYER REMINDER

For the eyes of the Lord are on the righteous
and his ears are attentive to their prayer.

—1 Peter 3:12

The Serenity Prayer

BY REINHOLD NIEBUHR

Serenity, *courage*, and *wisdom* are really big words. Let's bring them down to size. *Serenity* means having peace, no matter what is happening around you. *Courage* is doing what is right, even when you are afraid. And *wisdom* is doing things God's way. In this prayer, we ask God to give us serenity, courage, and wisdom.

> Lord, grant me the serenity
> To accept the things I cannot change,
> The courage to change the things I can,
> And the wisdom to know the difference.

When you need serenity, wisdom, or courage, ask God for it. He's always ready to answer that kind of prayer!

MY LITTLE PRAYER REMINDER

Courage is fear that has said its prayers.

—Dorothy Bernard

The Prayer of Abram

Abram and Sarai had grown old waiting for a child. So many years ago God had promised to give them a child. Had God forgotten them? Abram knelt and prayed:

"O Sovereign LORD, what can you give me since I remain childless?"

—Genesis 15:2

God had a surprising answer for Abram. "Count the stars. That's how many children you will have." And not long after that, baby Isaac was born! So what can God give? Anything!

MY LITTLE PRAYER REMINDER

Pray as though everything depended on God.
Work as though everything depended on you.

—St. Augustine

All Things Bright and Beautiful

BY CECIL FRANCIS ALEXANDER

Have you ever seen a monkey's lips? Don't laugh! Monkeys have great big lips! They use those lips to "yakity-yak" all day long. But they never say one word you can understand. Lots of animals have lips. But only people use their lips to form words. And words can say prayers!

All things bright and beautiful,
All creatures great and small,
All things wise and wonderful,
The Lord God made them all.

He gave us eyes to see them,
And lips that we might tell,
How great is God Almighty,
Who has made all things well.

Do you have lips? Of course you do! So use your lips to pray.

MY LITTLE PRAYER REMINDER

We must pray not, first of all, because it feels good or helps us,
but because God loves us and wants our attention.

—Henri J. M. Nouwen

What can I Give Him?

by Christina Rossetti

God has given us so many things. He's given us life and love. He's given us a beautiful world to live in. He has even sent His Son to save us. Sometimes I wish I could give God something to thank Him for all He's done. But what can I give Him?

> What can I give Him,
> Poor as I am?
> If I were a shepherd,
> I would bring a lamb.
>
> If I were a wise man,
> I would do my part.
> Yet what can I give Him?
> Give my heart.

When you give your heart to someone, it says, "I love you." So what can you give to God? You can give Him your heart!

WITH ALL MY HEART (I WILL PRAISE YOU)

CD 1
SONG 5

MY LITTLE PRAYER REMINDER

We must move from asking God to take care of the things that are breaking
our hearts, to praying about the things that are breaking His heart.

—Margaret Gibb

The Prayer of Jacob

— A PRAYER FOR PEACE —

Jacob and Esau were twins. Esau was the oldest. He would get the family blessing. At least that's how it *should* have been. But Jacob tricked his father, and he took the blessing. Not fair! Esau was very angry, and Jacob ran away. Years later the two brothers were about to meet again. So Jacob prayed:

"Save me, I pray, from the hand of my brother Esau, for I am afraid he will come and attack me."

—Genesis 32:11

Jacob's prayer was answered. Esau forgave him.

My Little Prayer Reminder

The power of prayer can never be overrated.

—Charles Spurgeon

17

A School Day Prayer

Some little kids have really big hurts. Yet day after day they go to school. They keep their hurts a secret. But Jesus knows all about their hurts. And He wants to heal them. Those kids need a kind word—from you!

Be with me, Lord, throughout the day.
Give me healing words to say
To the one who's sad and blue,
And needs a friend to help them through.
Lord, my heart has Your love in it.
So help me live for You each minute.
And when my day at school is through
May all that's done, be done for You.

Someone at your school may have asked God for a friend. *You* could be that friend. Just think, God might use you to answer someone's prayer!

My Little Prayer Reminder

The angel fetched Peter out of prison,
but it was prayer that fetched the angel.

—Thomas Watson

Day by Day

ADAPTED FROM A PRAYER BY RICHARD OF CHICHESTER

Friends love to talk. They talk at school. They talk on the phone. They talk just about anywhere! Day by day, friends talk about their hopes and dreams. God loves to talk with us too. That's called *prayer*! He wants us to share our hopes and dreams with Him.

Day by day, O Lord, three things I pray:
To see Thee more clearly,
Love Thee more dearly,
Follow Thee more nearly,
Day by day.

Always, stay in touch with your heavenly Father. Not because He doesn't already know all about you. But because you need to know all about Him!

O HAPPY DAY!
CD 1
SONG 8

My Little Prayer Reminder

Spend hours in prayer.

—Andrew A. Bonar

The Prayer of Deborah

Deborah was a judge in Israel. Everyone came to her for advice. One day a mighty enemy came to fight Israel. The people were so afraid, but Deborah was wise! She prayed. God answered, saying, "I will give you victory!" (from Judges 4:7). Israel fought and won. Deborah's happiness overflowed into a song of prayer and praise:

"I will sing to the LORD, I will sing;
I will make music to the LORD, the God of Israel."
—Judges 5:3

Are you feeling happy? Then sing to the Lord!

DEBORAH'S SONG: I WILL SING TO THE LORD

CD 1
SONG
9

MY LITTLE PRAYER REMINDER

Prayer strikes the winning blow.

—S. D. Gordon

A Prayer for My Family

God has created some pretty big things. Let's start with the earth and sky. Big! Let's not forget the sun and the moon. Really big! But His greatest creation was a man named Adam and a woman called Eve. They were the very first family.

God made you,
God made me.
He placed us in a family.
He loves each one,
And so should we.
O thank You, Lord,
For my family.

Prayer should be an important part of any family! It lets us talk to our really big God!

MY LITTLE PRAYER REMINDER

I remember my mother's prayers and they have always followed me.

—Abraham Lincoln

Morning Prayer

———— ADAPTED FROM A PRAYER BY MARTIN LUTHER ————

What's the first thing you think of in the morning? Pancakes? Soccer practice? Most days we think of ourselves first. But before you get all caught up in "I," "me," and "my," try to remember Him! Before you think about all the things *you* need to do, think about all that *God* has done—and thank Him!

We give thanks to You, heavenly Father,
through Jesus Christ Your Son,
that You protect us through the night
from all danger and harm.

We ask You to keep us this day
from wrong we may do,
that in thought, word, and deed
we may serve and please You.

Tomorrow morning, before the pancakes, pour out your prayers to God . . . then pour on the syrup!

MY LITTLE PRAYER REMINDER

He who runs from God in the morning will
scarcely find Him the rest of the day.

—John Bunyan

The Prayer of Samson

Because of God's favor, Samson grew to be the world's strongest man. But when he disobeyed God, Samson lost God's blessing of strength and was captured by his enemies. So Samson prayed:

"O Sovereign LORD, remember me. O God, please strengthen me just once more."
—Judges 16:28

God heard Samson's prayer, and his strength returned. Samson's enemies had chained him to a stone temple. But with a mighty push, down came that awful place. When you are feeling weak, remember Samson and pray to God who is strong!

MY LITTLE PRAYER REMINDER

Prayer breaks all bars, dissolves all chains, opens all prisons.

—E. M. Bounds

We Thank You, Lord

If you're like me, you love ice cream! And where does it come from? No, not from Eskimos! Or from stores, either. Everything we eat comes from tiny seeds made by God. That's why we thank Him!

We thank You, Lord, for happy hearts,
For rain and sunny weather.
Thank You, Father, for this food
And that we are together.
—Traditional

So next time you dig into a big cone of ice cream, thank God for tiny seeds. Why? Because ice cream is made from milk. Milk comes from cows. Cows eat grass, and grass comes from seeds. And seeds . . . well, you know where they come from!

MY LITTLE PRAYER REMINDER

Take time to pray. "The great big freight trains . . .
are never too busy to stop for fuel."

—M. E. Andross

Evening Prayer

ADAPTED FROM A PRAYER BY Martin Luther

There's a happy little song I love to sing. The words say, "He's got the whole world in His hands." Those must be some mighty big hands! The song tells of God's protection. You can place your life in His hands, all your hopes and fears. His hands will cover you and keep you safe.

We thank You, Father, through Jesus Your Son,
That You graciously protect us each day.
Forgive us the wrong which we have done.
Defend us from all dangers of this night.
Into Your hands we commit all that is ours,
And let Your angels have charge of us.

God's got the whole world—and that includes you—in His hands! Say this prayer to thank Him for His care.

MY LITTLE PRAYER REMINDER

God gave you a gift of 86,400 seconds today.

Have you used one to say "thank you"?

—William Arthur Ward

The Prayer of Hannah

Tears were falling from her eyes. Hannah wanted a child more than anything, but she had none. So sad! Hannah knelt before the Lord. She prayed out loud. The Lord answered Hannah by giving her a beautiful baby boy. So Hannah prayed:

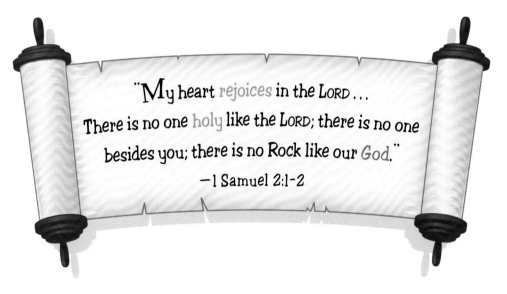

"My heart rejoices in the Lord . . .
There is no one holy like the Lord; there is no one besides you; there is no Rock like our God."
—1 Samuel 2:1-2

Hannah prayed out loud to the only One who could help her. Whether you pray out loud or in your thoughts, God always hears you.

HANNAH'S SONG: NO ONE HOLY LIKE THE LORD
CD 1
SONG 15

"Ask and it will be given to you."

—Matthew 7:7

The Peanut Butter Prayer

It was the third day of creation. God had made the earth and the sky. Busy day! He was now ready for plants. I think God had me in mind when He created that marvelous plant called the *peanut*. He said, "It is good." And I agree!

Lord, many wonders
Your hands have made;
The sun to shine brightly,
Trees to give shade.
But the wonder of wonders
Made like no other
Is jelly spread thick
On good peanut butter!

God made grapes for jelly, and wheat to grow grain for bread. And then, wonder of wonders, the peanut. Put them all together, and you get one of God's gifts to the world: the peanut butter sandwich!

MY LITTLE PRAYER REMINDER

He can do all things who prays well.

—G. F. Oliver

The Peace Prayer

BY ST. FRANCIS OF ASSISI

What does it mean to be an instrument? A piano is a musical instrument. A musician uses the piano to make music. A hammer is a builder's instrument. A builder uses the hammer to make a house. You become an instrument of God when He uses you to build His kingdom!

Lord, make me an instrument of Your peace.
Where there is hatred, let me sow love;
Where there is injury, pardon;
Where there is doubt, faith;
Where there is despair, hope;
Where there is darkness, light;
And where there is sadness, joy.

When God uses you, something good always happens. Isn't it wonderful to know that God can use you to build His kingdom? That's the reason He made you!

MY LITTLE PRAYER REMINDER

Prayer is music in the ears of God.

—Daniel Pledge

The Prayer of Solomon

A Prayer of Worship

Solomon was the wisest man who ever lived. He became king of Israel when his father, David, died. He built a temple to honor God. Very wise! The temple was a place to worship God. On the day the temple was dedicated, Solomon prayed:

"O Lord, God of Israel, there is no God like you in heaven above or on earth below — you who keep your covenant of love."

—1 Kings 8:23

We *worship* whatever rules our time, thoughts, and choices. Only God should be worshiped. Worship the Lord with your time, thoughts, and prayers!

My Little Prayer Reminder

Worship the Lord your God and serve him only.

—Luke 4:8

When I Grow up

Surprise parties are such fun! One minute everything is quiet. Then, "Surprise!" All of your friends jump out and the party begins. Everyone is surprised. Everyone but God. He's never surprised! God knows your yesterday, your today, and your tomorrow. And He has a plan for your life.

When I grow up, what will I be?
I wonder, Lord, what's planned for me;
A mission field so far away,
Or working here with friends each day?

Lord, You know what lies ahead,
So I'll just snuggle in my bed
And trust You as my life unfolds,
Knowing, God, You're in control.

Ask God to show you His plan for your life—and then prepare to be surprised by the great things He will do!

HE IS LORD!
CD 1
SONG 19

Don't pray when you feel like it.

Have an appointment with the Lord and keep it.

—Corrie Ten Boom

The Universal Prayer

BY CLEMENT XI

Obedience is doing what you are asked to do. Everyone should obey God. We should do whatever He asks, for as long as He asks, whenever He asks. Anything else is called *disobedience*.

Guide me by Your wisdom,
Correct me with Your justice,
Comfort me with Your mercy,
Protect me with Your power....

I want to do what You ask of me:
In the way You ask,
For as long as You ask,
Because You ask it.

Jesus taught about love. People who love Him obey Him. Show Jesus how much you love Him by doing what He asks you to do. Show Mom and Dad by obeying them too!

MY LITTLE PRAYER REMINDER

God speaks in the silence of the heart.

Listening is the beginning of prayer.

—Mother Teresa

The Prayer of Elijah

There they stood. The 450 priests of Baal on one side and Elijah on the other. Baal was a false god. He had no power at all. But Elijah's God was real. He was the one true God. Elijah laughed at Baal and prayed:

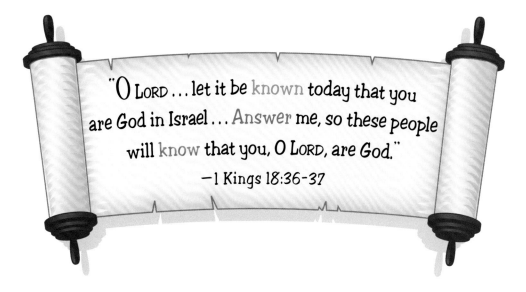

"O LORD . . . let it be known today that you are God in Israel . . . Answer me, so these people will know that you, O LORD, are God."
—1 Kings 18:36-37

At that very moment, God answered. Fire fell from heaven! The sacrifice, the wood, even the stones of the altar were burned up. Only the one true God answers prayer. And He will answer yours!

MY LITTLE PRAYER REMINDER

You may as soon find a living man that does not breathe,
as a living Christian that does not pray.

—Matthew Henry

Rainy Days

Rain can ruin a baseball game or a day at the beach. But a farmer doesn't complain. He loves the rain! It makes his crops grow and gives his cows a drink. It all depends on how you look at it!

Lord, I'm thankful
When rainy days come,
'Cause rain makes puddles
And puddles are fun!

I love to splish
And splash away.
But Mom prefers
A sunny day.

Puddles—some people see them as something to step over. But kids see them as "showers of blessing" and splash right through the middle! It's all how you look at it.

MY LITTLE PRAYER REMINDER

Don't pray when it rains if you don't pray when the sun shines.

—Satchel Paige

Footprints

Jesus walked along the shores of the Sea of Galilee. There He saw Peter, Andrew, James, and John. They were fishermen. He said to them, "Come, follow Me." What did He mean? Was this a new game of "Follow the Leader"?

> May we be able to follow
> In the footprints of Your beloved Son,
> Our Lord Jesus Christ,
> And, by Your grace alone,
> May we make our way to You.

Jesus wasn't playing a game, but He was being the Leader. Peter, Andrew, James, and John followed Jesus all their lives. That's what Jesus wants from you too!

COME AND SEE
CD 1
SONG 23

My Little Prayer Reminder

Just pray for a tough hide and a tender heart.

—Ruth Graham

The Prayer of Jabez

A Prayer for God's Blessing

Jabez was a good man. He loved the Lord. He knew that all blessings come from Him. So he asked God for a blessing. Jabez knew that God was a listening God. He would hear his prayer and answer. Jabez prayed:

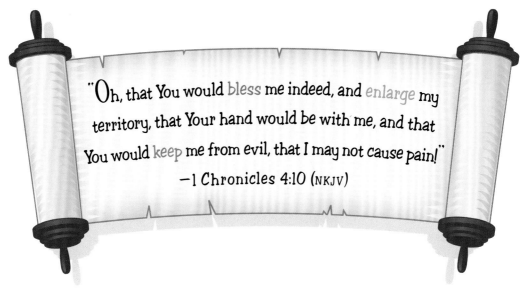

"Oh, that You would bless me indeed, and enlarge my territory, that Your hand would be with me, and that You would keep me from evil, that I may not cause pain!"
—1 Chronicles 4:10 (NKJV)

The prayer of Jabez pleased God because he prayed for others.

MY LITTLE PRAYER REMINDER

God shapes the world by prayer.

—E. M. Bounds

Thank You

When should you say "thank you"? That's easy! You say "thank you" when someone does a nice thing for you. God has done something nicer than nice! He's done something awesome! He created a world full of wonderful blessings. So you can pray:

Thank You for the world so sweet,
Thank You for the food we eat.
Thank You for the birds that sing,
Thank You, God, for everything.
—Traditional

God created all things. So thank Him for everything! Can you think of three things you are thankful for?

MY LITTLE PRAYER REMINDER

If the only prayer you ever say in your whole life
is "thank you," that would be enough!

—Meister Eckhart

Turning to God

by Abraham Lincoln

Our nation was once torn apart by the Civil War. Americans were fighting Americans. Where did President Lincoln turn in this time of deep distress? To God in prayer! Kneeling before an open Bible, Abraham Lincoln prayed:

> Oh, God, who heard Solomon in the night
> when he prayed and cried for wisdom,
> oh, God, hear me.
> I cannot guide the affairs of this nation
> without Your help.
> Hear me and save this nation.

Today, our country faces troubled times. Like Abraham Lincoln, we should turn to God. God says that if His people will humble themselves and pray, He will hear from heaven and heal their land (from 2 Chronicles 7:14).

MY LITTLE PRAYER REMINDER

Continue in prayer until we obtain an answer.

—George Müller

The Prayer of Asa

Asa was a good king. When a strong army came to fight Israel, he prayed. He knew that Israel needed God's help. So Asa put his life and the lives of his men in God's care. On the day Israel's army prepared for battle, Asa prayed:

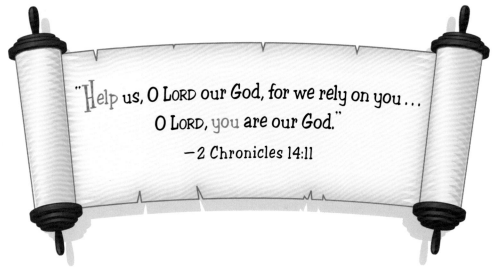

"Help us, O LORD our God, for we rely on you . . . O LORD, you are our God."

—2 Chronicles 14:11

When you need a little help, that's the best thing you can do too. Pray and trust God to take care of you. Then do your best. God will help you too!

MY LITTLE PRAYER REMINDER

If I could hear Christ praying for me in the next room,
I would not fear a million enemies!

—Robert Murray M'Cheyne

The Puppy Prayer

God answers every prayer. Some He answers quickly, like Jonah's prayer.
Some answers take a long time, like Abram and Sarai's.

Lord, this prayer, Mom may contest,
But one of us will be so blessed.
You always do the thing that's right,
So hear this prayer I pray tonight.
I saw this puppy at the mall —
The cutest pup I ever saw!
The sign said free — what a deal!
I'll love him, Lord, You know I will!
Mom said, "Maybe." So, Lord, please bless,
Turn her "Maybe" to a "Yes!"
But if my hope she does decline,
I pray that Dad might change her mind!

Prayer is not getting what *you* want; it is wanting what *God* gives you.

MY LITTLE PRAYER REMINDER

Prayer is not to influence God, but rather to change … the one who prays.

—Soren Kierkegaard

Shine Through Us

— BY JOHN HENRY NEWMAN, AS QUOTED BY MOTHER TERESA —

There is a song I love to sing. It says, "This little light of mine. I'm gonna let it shine, let it shine, let it shine, let it shine." What kind of light are we singing about? It is the light of Jesus! It shines out of the heart of every believer.

Dear Jesus, shine through us, and be so in us.
That every soul we come in contact with may feel Your presence in our soul…
Stay with us, and then we shall begin to shine as You shine,
So to shine as to be light to others.

The light, O Jesus, will be all from You, none of it will be ours.
It will be You shining on others through us.
Let us thus praise You in the way You love best,
By shining on those around us.

You can shine like a candle in a dark room when you tell others about God's love. So let your little light shine!

MY LITTLE PRAYER REMINDER

One tiny candle may lead a thousand out of darkness.

The Prayer of Jehoshaphat

No one had ever seen so many soldiers before! Thousands had come to fight against Israel. They looked mean and ready for battle. Yikes! Jehoshaphat was afraid. With a large army ready to attack, what did he do *first*? Make a new battle plan? Run away? No! He called all the people together—men, women, and children—and *prayed!*

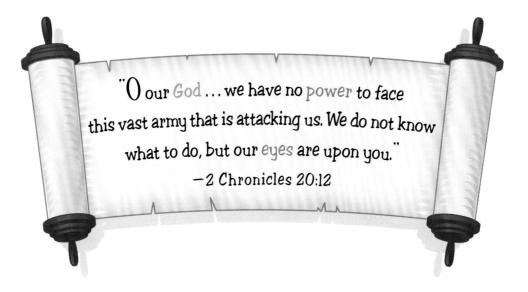

"O our God . . . we have no power to face this vast army that is attacking us. We do not know what to do, but our eyes are upon you."

—2 Chronicles 20:12

God answered Jehoshaphat, saying, "The battle is mine!" (from 2 Chronicles 20:15). So when you don't know what to do, pray *first!*

JEHOSHAPHAT'S SONG: WE SHOULD PRAY

CD 1
SONG 30

MY LITTLE PRAYER REMINDER

The trouble with our praying is, we just do it as a means of last resort.

—Will Rogers

Jesus, Tender Savior

I love going to church where I can learn about Jesus. Do you know why? Without Jesus, I would be lost in sin and separated from God. We all would! But God loves us so much He sent Jesus, His perfect Son to die for us so we could be with Him forever.

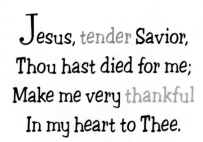

Jesus, tender Savior,
Thou hast died for me;
Make me very thankful
In my heart to Thee.

Soon I hope in glory
At Thy side to stand;
Make me fit to meet Thee
In that happy land!

—Traditional

Jesus has done something only He could do. He gave His life for me to save me from sin.

JESUS LOVES ME

CD 1
SONG 31

MY LITTLE PRAYER REMINDER

Everything starts with prayer.

—Mother Teresa

I Am Thine, O Lord

BY FANNY CROSBY

Have you ever belonged to a club? I was once a scout. I learned to tie knots and paddle a canoe. Fun! *Belong* can mean "to be a part of." But *belong* can also mean "to own"—like "that toy *belongs* to me." When you believe in Jesus, you *belong* to Him.

I am Thine, O Lord,
I have heard Thy voice,
And it told of Thy love for me;
But I long to rise in the arms of faith
And be closer drawn to Thee.

When you belong to Jesus, He will love you and take care of you!

I AM THINE, O LORD

CD 1 SONG 32

My Little Prayer Reminder

Belonging to God is the greatest freedom of all.

The Prayer of Nehemiah

A PRAYER FOR SUCCESS

Nehemiah wept. Word came that the wall of Jerusalem was broken down. The gates were burned. Nehemiah wanted to rebuild the wall. But he could not go without the king's permission. So Nehemiah prayed:

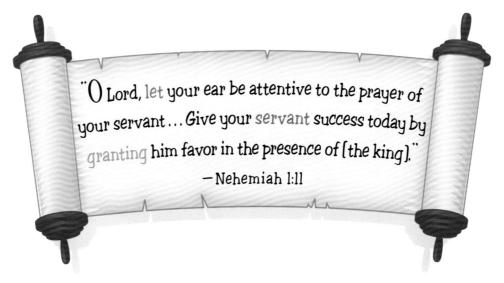

"O Lord, let your ear be attentive to the prayer of your servant... Give your servant success today by granting him favor in the presence of [the king]."
—Nehemiah 1:11

When the king said, "Yes, you can go," Nehemiah knew God had answered his prayer. He would work with those who honored God to rebuild Jerusalem's wall. God gave Nehemiah success! So before you go to work for God, pray first!

MY LITTLE PRAYER REMINDER

One should never start anything that he cannot cover with prayer.

—Unknown

Two Little Eyes

God wants you to have a willing heart. That means you serve Him because you *want to*, not because you *have to*. Willingly use your eyes and ears to serve Him. How happy God is to hear this prayer!

Two little eyes to look to God;
Two little ears to hear His Word;
Two little feet to walk in His ways;
Two little lips to sing His praise;
Two little hands to do His will;
One little heart to love Him still.

—Traditional

God wants you to serve Him. It's not always easy. You may be asked to do something you've never done before—like tell a friend about Jesus. But if you are willing, God will be with you!

MY LITTLE PRAYER REMINDER

Prayer is where the action is.

—John Wesley

Most Richly Blessed

—— PRAYER OF AN UNKNOWN CIVIL WAR SOLDIER ——

Wouldn't it be nice if God would give you everything you asked for? Just think, you could have all new toys, Disneyland every day, and a million dollars! And we're just getting started. Oops! God isn't a genie in a bottle who just gives you what *you* want.

I asked for riches, that I might be happy;
I was given poverty, that I might be wise.

I asked for power, that I might have the praise of men;
I was given weakness, that I might feel the need of God.

I asked for all things, that I might enjoy life;
I was given life, that I might enjoy all things.

I got nothing that I asked for, but everything I had hoped for.
Almost despite myself, my unspoken prayers were answered.

I am, among all men, most richly blessed.

Trust God—even when He says "no" to what you want. He knows what's best for you.

There are four ways God answers prayer: No, not yet; No, I love you too much;
Yes, I thought you'd never ask; Yes, and here's more.

—Anne Lewis

A Shepherd's Prayer

David is called the shepherd king. As a boy, he spent many nights tending sheep on lonely hillsides. He marveled as he looked up into the starlit sky. He wanted every thought to please the Creator. David prayed:

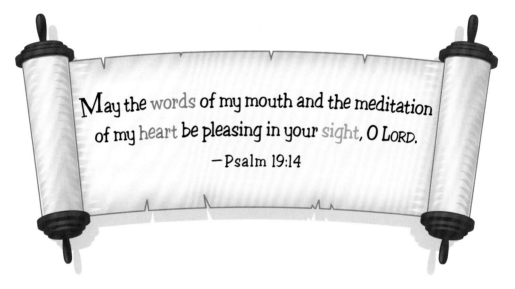

May the words of my mouth and the meditation of my heart be pleasing in your sight, O LORD.

—Psalm 19:14

How can you please God? Love Him. Trust Him. Obey Him. Then you will be pleasing in His sight.

MY LITTLE PRAYER REMINDER

When at night you cannot sleep, talk to the Shepherd and stop counting sheep.

—Unknown

A Penny Prayer

Every time you hand a penny to someone, guess what happens? You are passing along a prayer! That's right. A very special prayer is written on the face of every penny. Do you know what that penny prayer says?

This little penny's not worth much.
It won't buy diamonds, pearls, and such.
But upon its face is written there,
A nation's hope, a timeless prayer.

It's e'er so small as it can be;
"In God we trust" is all you see.
But it says to all, God will be
The One we trust for liberty!

The penny prayer says, "Lord, I believe Your promises. I trust You to guide our nation." Trust God . . . for everything!

MY LITTLE PRAYER REMINDER

Faith and prayer are the vitamins of the soul;
man cannot live in health without them.

—Mahalia Jackson

Today

A SILLY DAY PRAYER

The psalmist wrote, "Make a joyful noise to the Lord" (from Psalm 66:1). When children laugh and play together, that's a joyful noise! It's strange to think that having fun together can be a part of God's plan. But it is! One of the fruits of the Spirit is *joy*!

Noisy planes go zoom, zoom, zoom!
Noisy drums go boom, boom, boom!
Noisy trains go clickety-clack!
Noisy people yakity-yak!

Lots of noises in my ear,
But there's one noise God loves to hear:
The sound of laughing girls and boys.
Thank You, Lord, for joyful noise!

Knowing that you are a child of God should put a great big smile on your face. So make a joyful noise. God will love it!

MY LITTLE PRAYER REMINDER

When you pray, things remain the same, but you begin to be different.

—Oswald Chambers

A Prayer of David

David was a shepherd who took care of his sheep. David trusted God to be his shepherd and take good care of him. So he wrote this prayer:

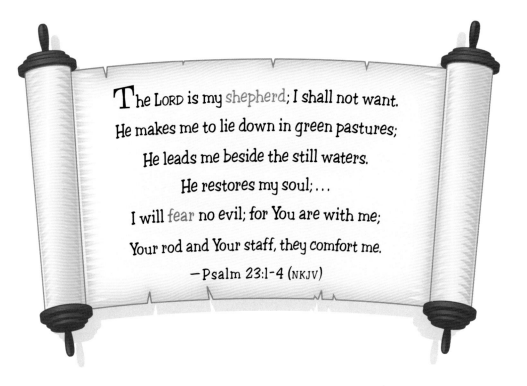

The LORD is my shepherd; I shall not want.
He makes me to lie down in green pastures;
He leads me beside the still waters.
He restores my soul; . . .
I will fear no evil; for You are with me;
Your rod and Your staff, they comfort me.
—Psalm 23:1–4 (NKJV)

God is our Shepherd, and we are His lambs. He guides us and He comforts us. He walks with us in dark places, so we need not fear. The Shepherd is always near.

My Little Prayer Reminder

Satan does not care how many people read about prayer
if only he can keep them from praying.

—Paul E. Billheimer

Seasons

Things are changing every day! Warm summer breezes turn cooler and autumn leaves fall. Cool winds turn cold and snowflakes fall. But before long, spring flowers pop up, and we praise God for April showers. Yes, everything changes . . . except the One who made it all!

Winter, spring,
Summer, and fall,
Lord, I know,
You made them all.

And though the seasons
Change, we see,
You are the same—
Eternally!

God is the same yesterday, today, and forever. His love for you never changes. His promises never fail. That's because God never changes!

MY LITTLE PRAYER REMINDER

Time spent alone with God is not wasted.

—M. E. Andross

Be Near Me, Lord Jesus

BY JOHN T. MCFARLAND

The moon is more than 238,000 miles away from where you are. Wow! That's a long way! Some people think God is even farther away than the moon. But the Bible says that God is near. He is near to all who call upon Him.

> Be near me, Lord Jesus, I ask Thee to stay
> Close by me forever, and love me, I pray.
> Bless all the dear children in Thy tender care,
> And fit us for heaven to live with Thee there.

Do you know why God stays so close? Because He loves you! The God who created that faraway moon loves you! He wants to be your closest friend!

BE NEAR ME, LORD JESUS

CD 1
SONG 41

MY LITTLE PRAYER REMINDER

God is as close to you as a prayer.

David's Prayer

David disobeyed God. He was very sorry. He wanted to be forgiven. So he prayed. He asked the Lord to change his heart. He wanted to feel the joy that comes from doing the right thing.

Create in me a pure heart, O God...

Restore to me the joy of your salvation

and grant me a willing spirit, to sustain me.

—Psalm 51:10, 12

No matter what you have done, God still loves you. So when you feel sorry for something you've done, find a quiet place, pray, and ask God to forgive you. He always will!

MY LITTLE PRAYER REMINDER

Every great movement of God can be traced to a kneeling figure.

—D. L. Moody

Now I Lay Me Down to Sleep

Were you ever asked to *keep* something? Maybe you kept a puppy while a friend was away. Puppies can be lots of fun. But that little pup depends on you. You must feed him and keep him safe. That's what a keeper does!

> Now I lay me down to sleep,
> I pray the Lord my soul to keep.
> Keep me safely through the night,
> And wake me with the morning light.
> —Traditional

The Lord is your keeper. He takes care of you. He watches over you as you sleep. That's because He loves you.

MY LITTLE PRAYER REMINDER

Prayer should be the key of the day and the lock of the night.

—George Herbert

He Prayeth Well

BY SAMUEL TAYLOR COLERIDGE

God is love. You can't have one without the other. If God is there, love is there too! That's why Christians should love people. Now, I'm not talking about a handshake and a "howdy-do." I'm talking about the kind of love that begins with God and ends with service.

He prays well, who loves well
Both man and bird and beast.
He prays best, who loves best
All things both great and small;
For the dear God who loves us,
He made and loves all.

What does it mean to "love well"? It means to love God with all your heart. And that kind of love always leads you to serve others.

KEEP ON LOVIN'
CD 1
SONG 44

MY LITTLE PRAYER REMINDER

The value of . . . prayer is not that God will hear us,

but that we will hear Him.

—William McGill

The Prayer of Ethan

Ethan knew that God was faithful. God always does what He says He will do. That's what being faithful means. So Ethan was confused. God had promised Israel the victory, but they had lost the battle. Why? Ethan didn't understand God, but still he trusted. Ethan prayed:

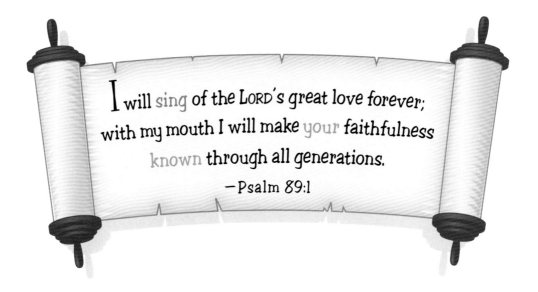

I will sing of the LORD's great love forever;
with my mouth I will make your faithfulness
known through all generations.

−Psalm 89:1

When you don't understand what God is doing—pray! God will be faithful to you too! Only trust Him!

MY LITTLE PRAYER REMINDER

God's faithfulness is never so evident as to the one who is faithful to pray.

God, Hear My Prayer

A-Choo! Bless you! A blessing is more than words we say when we sneeze. A prayer blessing is like giving someone a little push. Like a propeller on a boat, prayer blessings push us forward. They encourage us to keep going.

God in heaven, hear my prayer,
Keep me in Thy loving care.
Be my guide in all I do,
Bless all those who love me too.
—Traditional

When we pray for others, God is pleased! Maybe someone you know needs a prayer blessing right now.

MY LITTLE PRAYER REMINDER

The greatest thing anyone can do for God and man is to pray.

—S. D. Gordon

Your Glory

BY MICHELANGELO

When we give God "glory," we give Him credit for all He's done. At the end of a movie, we see the movie makers' names. Those are called the *credits*. But God made something much greater than a movie! God made everything. For that, we give Him all the glory.

Lord, make me see Your glory in every place.

Only God can create life. Only God can speak and make a world appear. Only God can save the lost. Praise God in your prayers, and give Him all the credit—I mean *glory*!

MY LITTLE PRAYER REMINDER

Prayer does not fit us for the greater work; prayer is the greater work.

—Oswald Chambers

The Prayer of Moses

A *dwelling place* is where families live. It is a strong house that shelters us from storms. It is the place we run to when the rain falls. Most importantly, it is the place where we are loved. God is all of these things. That's why Moses prayed:

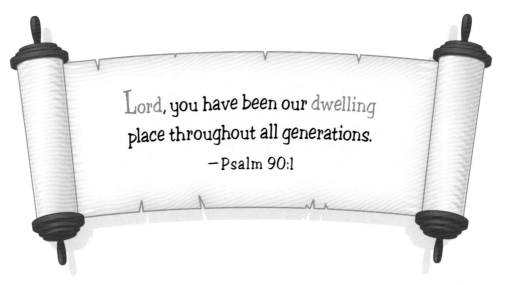

Lord, you have been our dwelling place throughout all generations.

—Psalm 90:1

God is our shelter from the storm. He is the One we run to when we are troubled. He is that special place of love and peace. So, come on in! God is our dwelling place.

My Little Prayer Reminder

Prayer is a strong wall and fortress of the church.

—Martin Luther

Another Year Is Dawning

BY FRANCES HAVERGAL

"Happy New Year!" we shout. The old year is gone and a new one is here. Do you know what makes a new year "happy"? It all starts with prayer. We thank God for all He has done. Then we ask Him to bless the coming year.

Another year is dawning
Dear Father, let it be
In working or in waiting
Another year with Thee.

Another year of progress,
Another year of praise,
Another year of proving
Thy presence all the days.

No one knows what the future holds—not the tiniest baby or the oldest man. But God does! So begin every new year—and every new day—with prayer!

MY LITTLE PRAYER REMINDER

If God orders each and every step of your future,
you may want to talk to Him about the schedule.

A Family Prayer

BY ROBERT LOUIS STEVENSON

Joshua once said, "As for me and my household, we will serve the LORD" (Joshua 24:15). Not only had Joshua decided to serve God, he wanted his whole family to serve Him. Praying together is an important part of serving.

Lord, behold our family here assembled.
We thank Thee for this place in which we dwell;
For the love that unites us;
For the peace accorded to us this day;

For the hope with which we expect the morrow;
For the health, the work, the food, and the bright skies
That make our lives delightful;
For our friends in all parts of the earth.

Does your family pray together? If not, start today. Pray at mealtime, at bedtime, or after school. Prayer is like glue: it holds families together!

CHOOSE
CD 1
SONG 50

MY LITTLE PRAYER REMINDER

Nothing holds a family together like praying parents.

The Prayer of Jeremiah

Prayer changes things. Jeremiah believed this. So why was he weeping? He wept because Israel would not obey God. He asked the people to change, but they would not. So he prayed:

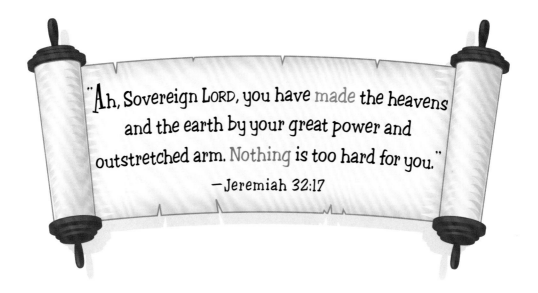

"Ah, Sovereign LORD, you have made the heavens and the earth by your great power and outstretched arm. Nothing is too hard for you."
—Jeremiah 32:17

Jeremiah knew that prayer changes things. So he prayed for Israel to change and to return to God. Our nation needs to return to God too. So let's all pray for our nation, just like Jeremiah did!

MY LITTLE PRAYER REMINDER

We are one nation under God, so let prayer rise up to Him.

Mama's Little House

When a baby is born, he moves out of Mama's tummy into God's big world. He is just the same one minute *before* being born as he is one minute *after*.

Mama's little house is my dwelling place,
Made by God, with just the right space.
I'll not be here long, by God's design,
I'll trade Mama's house, for the bright sunshine.

Thank you dear Father for life and your love.
I'm growing, just knowing you'll watch from above
When I first hug mama, and say my first prayer
And see my first rainbow and breathe my first air.

Till then, I'll be here, snuggled away
In Mama's little house, awaiting the day
When I will trade spaces, born to the light,
A child of my Father, forever ... good night!

Both Mama's tummy (her little house) and the world are places made by God and full of love.

CRADLE HYMN
CD 2
SONG 2

My Little Prayer Reminder

The most important thing a born again Christian can do is to pray.

—Chuck Smith

The Lord Is Good to Me

ATTRIBUTED TO JOHNNY APPLESEED

People knew him as Johnny Appleseed. His real name was John Chapman. He is famous for planting apple trees throughout the Ohio area. But did you know that he was a missionary too? He had a great love for God's creation. This simple pioneer once prayed:

Oh, the Lord is good to me,
And so I thank the Lord
For giving me the things I need:
The sun, the rain, and the apple seed.
Oh, the Lord is good to me.

God's goodness is found in simple things—like apples, sunshine, and rain. Thank God for all the simple blessings that show His goodness!

MY LITTLE PRAYER REMINDER

Little prayers are like little seeds.
Once planted, they bring forth the fruit of blessing.

A Prayer of Daniel

A PRAYER FOR MERCY

How deep is God's love? It's very deep. No matter how much He pours out, there's always more. God poured out His saving love on Daniel. Remember that hungry den of lions? God saved Daniel. In this prayer, Daniel pours out his love to the Lord:

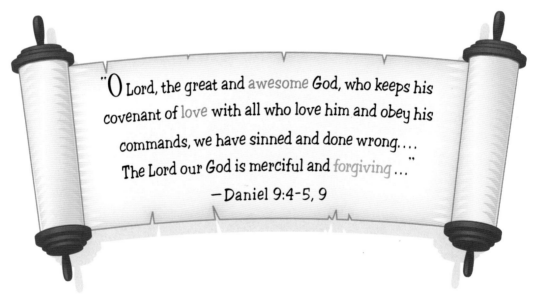

"O Lord, the great and awesome God, who keeps his covenant of love with all who love him and obey his commands, we have sinned and done wrong.... The Lord our God is merciful and forgiving..."

—Daniel 9:4-5, 9

A *covenant* is a promise. God promises to love us. And that's a promise He will never break!

MY LITTLE PRAYER REMINDER

What a privilege to carry everything to God in prayer!

—Joseph Scriven

Day Is Done

David was a shepherd boy. He watched over the sheep at night. Sheep say, "Baa!" He kept them safe from wolves and bears. Bears say, "Grrr!" When David felt afraid, he would pray. If you are afraid, you can pray too!

> Day is done,
> Gone the sun,
> From the lakes,
> From the hills,
>
> From the sky.
> All is well,
> Safe at rest.
> God is nigh.
> —Unknown

David trusted in God, who is stronger than wolves and bears! And you can too!

MY LITTLE PRAYER REMINDER

Pray, and let God worry.

—Martin Luther

My Heart

BY GEORGE HERBERT

The Bible speaks of *faith*, *hope*, and *charity*. *Faith* is believing in God, though you cannot see Him. *Hope* is knowing that God will do what He says. *Charity* is loving God by serving others.

> Enrich my heart, mouth, hands in me,
> With faith, with hope, with charity,
> That I may run, rise, rest with Thee.

Prayer keeps us close to God. So when you wake up each morning, pray! As you go through a busy day, pray! And at bedtime, pray!

MY LITTLE PRAYER REMINDER

Prayer is asking for the rain and faith is carrying the umbrella.

—Anonymous

The Prayer of Jonah

God told Jonah to go and preach in Nineveh. So where did he go? He set sail for Tarshish! But God has a "whale" of a way of changing minds when we disobey. A great storm came up, Jonah went down, and there he prayed, inside the belly of a giant fish!

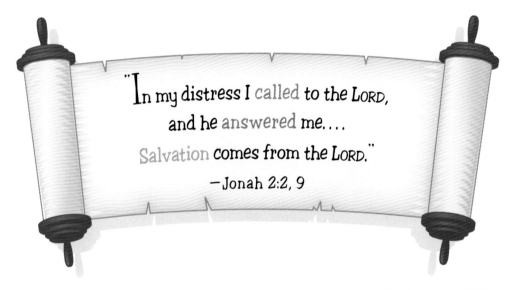

"In my distress I called to the LORD,
and he answered me....
Salvation comes from the LORD."

—Jonah 2:2, 9

When God says do *this*, but you do *that*, you can find yourself in an awful mess. But remember Jonah and choose to pray—no matter where you are!

MY LITTLE PRAYER REMINDER

The only power that God will yield to is that of prayer.

—Leonard Ravenhill

Jesus, Friend of Little children

BY WALTER J. MATHAMS

It's great fun having a friend over to play. The time passes so quickly. You wish your friend could stay forever! Did you know you have a friend like that? A friend who never leaves!

> Jesus, friend of little children
> Be a friend to me;
> Take my hand, and ever keep me
> Close to Thee.
>
> Never leave me, nor forsake me;
> Ever be my friend;
> For I need Thee, from life's dawning
> To its end.

Jesus will never leave us or forsake us. He's a friend who can stay all day, all night, always!

MY LITTLE PRAYER REMINDER

Rich is the person who has a praying friend.

—Janice Hughes

Help Me, Lord

BY ROBERT LOUIS STEVENSON

"I want to do it myself!" Ever said that? Yes, there are lots of things you *can* do yourself. Like brushing your teeth or combing your hair. But there are some things you *can't* do by yourself. You need God to help you.

Help me, Lord, to love You more
Than I ever loved before.
In my work and in my play,
Please be with me through the day.

Now, before I run to play,
Let me not forget to pray
To God who kept me through the night
And waked me with the morning light.

When you ask, God will help. He will help you love Him more! He'll even help you think about yourself less and others more!

God of Our Fathers

CD 2
SONG 9

MY LITTLE PRAYER REMINDER

Prayer cuts the biggest problem down to size.

The Prayer of Micah

Micah was a prophet. He preached to those who were poor and without hope. He warned them that disobedience would lead to God's punishment. But he had some good news too! If they would turn back to God, they would be blessed. Micah prayed:

I watch in hope for the LORD, I wait for God my Savior; my God will hear me.

—Micah 7:7

In the Bible, *hope* is not just a wish. *Hope* is knowing for certain that the Lord hears and answers your prayers.

MY LITTLE PRAYER REMINDER

No man is greater than his prayer life.

—Leonard Ravenhill

A Child's Easter Prayer

A PRAYER ABOUT JELLY BEANS

The story of Jesus is the sweetest, most colorful story ever told. All that God has done for you and me can be seen in a jar of jelly beans.

Pure and white for God's own Son;
Yellow for the victory won.
Blue is for the pain He bore.
Green, the crown of thorns He wore.
Red, the blood He shed that day,
Black, the tomb where Jesus lay.
Orange, the color of morning sky,
Purple, for this King of mine.
Let each jelly bean proclaim
The glory of our Savior's name.
And may each color help us see
God's great love for you and me.

Jesus' story is the sweetest story of all!

CHRIST THE LORD HAS RISEN TODAY
CD 2
SONG 11

MY LITTLE PRAYER REMINDER

Be joyful in hope, patient in affliction, faithful in prayer.

—Romans 12:12

Grant to Us, O Lord

BY THOMAS À KEMPIS

Evil! That's a scary word. What does it mean to a kid? *Evil* is simply doing what *we* want to do, instead of doing what *God* has asked us to do. Remember Jonah? He did what he wanted to do (evil), not what God asked (good). That is what evil means.

Grant to us, O Lord,
To know that which is worth knowing,
To love that which is worth loving,
To praise that which pleases You most,
To esteem that which is most precious to You,
And to dislike what is evil in Your eyes.
Grant us true judgment to distinguish things that differ
And above all, to search out and do what is well pleasing to You,
Through Jesus Christ, our Lord. Amen.

Sometimes it's hard to be good. Ask God to give you the courage to do what is right. He will help you!

MY LITTLE PRAYER REMINDER

The prayer of a righteous man is powerful and effective.

—James 5:16

The Prayer of Habakkuk

A Prayer of Happiness

Habakkuk knew the secret of happiness. It's not found in the things we own or things that happen to us. Habakkuk said he would be happy even if "the fig tree does not bud and there are no grapes on the vines" (Habakkuk 3:17). What was this secret of happiness?

Yet I will rejoice in the LORD,
I will be joyful in God my Savior.

—Habakkuk 3:18

"Yet" is the secret. "Yet" says that no matter what happens, you choose to trust God. God is your happiness. That's the secret!

MY LITTLE PRAYER REMINDER

God will either give you what you ask, or something far better.

—Robert Murray M'Cheyne

My Little Tongue

Captains steer great big boats with a tiny rudder. You can't see it. It's under the boat. But it turns the whole ship. A rudder turned in the wrong direction can cause big problems. In the same way, your tongue can cause big problems if it says unkind things. So be careful what you say:

Lord, keep my little tongue today,
Keep it gentle while I play;
Keep my hands from doing wrong.
Keep my feet the whole day long.
Keep me all, O Jesus mild,
Keep me ever Thy dear child.

—Traditional

Ask God to guide all that you say, so that your words will be pleasing to Him and others.

MY LITTLE PRAYER REMINDER

The secret of praying is praying in secret.

—Leonard Ravenhill

I Arise Today

BY ST. PATRICK

Sometimes we get a little "too big for our britches." If we win the race, we take all the credit. If we make an "A" on the test, we brag a bit. But never forget, though we run, it is God who gives us the strength.

I arise today through God's strength to pilot me:

God's might to uphold me,
God's wisdom to guide me,
God's eye to look before me,
God's ear to hear me,

God's Word to speak for me,
God's hand to guard me,
God's way to lie before me,
God's shield to protect me.

God gives us everything. So remember to give Him all the thanks and praise.

MY LITTLE PRAYER REMINDER

Is prayer your steering wheel or your spare tire?

—Corrie Ten Boom

The Prayer of Ezra

The word *righteous* is a mighty big word. But it's easy to understand. Righteous people do what God says is right. The problem is, it's tough to be righteous all the time. Sometimes we do the wrong things. But God is righteous all the time. So when Israel disobeyed the Lord, Ezra prayed:

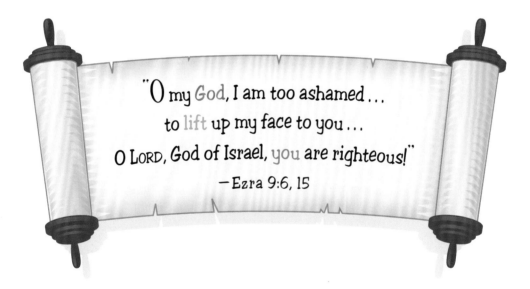

"O my God, I am too ashamed . . .
to lift up my face to you . . .
O LORD, God of Israel, you are righteous!"
—Ezra 9:6, 15

God is righteous all the time. He never says or does the wrong thing. That's why you can always trust Him.

MY LITTLE PRAYER REMINDER

Do not pray for easy lives. Pray to be stronger men!

—Phillips Brooks

A Child's Evening Prayer

GOD LISTENS TO OUR PRAYERS

When you pray, you have a little talk with God. Sometimes you talk and He listens. Other times, God talks and you listen. How does God speak? He speaks through the Bible, through His Holy Spirit, and through what is happening around you.

All this day Your hand has led me,
And I thank You for Your care;
You have warmed me, clothed me, fed me;
Listen to my evening prayer.

May my sins be all forgiven;
Bless the friends I love so well;
Take me, Lord, at last to heaven.
Happy there with You to dwell.

—Traditional

You don't have to know giant words to say a prayer. You just need a giant love for the One who listens and loves you so!

MY LITTLE PRAYER REMINDER

Seven days without prayer makes one weak.

—Allen E. Vartlett

The Forget-Me-Not Prayer

ADAPTED FROM A PRAYER BY Sir Jacob Astley

My dad once said that I would forget my head if it weren't attached! We all have moments when we forget important things. Sometimes we even forget to pray! Long ago one busy soldier prayed this prayer:

Oh Lord, You know how busy I must be this day; if I forget You, do not forget me.

Don't worry. The good news is that while you may sometimes forget to pray, God still watches over you. He never forgets His children!

MY LITTLE PRAYER REMINDER

There is not in the world a kind of life more sweet and delightful
than that of a continual conversation with God.

—Brother Lawrence

The Lord's Prayer

JESUS TAUGHT US TO PRAY

Many people had gathered on that mountainside. They had come to hear Jesus. He taught them many lessons about love and kindness. On this day, He taught them how to pray, saying:

"Our Father in heaven, hallowed be your name, your kingdom come, your will be done on earth as it is in heaven. Give us today our daily bread. Forgive us our debts, as we also have forgiven our debtors. And lead us not into temptation but deliver us from the evil one."

—Matthew 6:9-13

So when you pray, remember Jesus' example. Know who you are talking to—the Father. Praise and thank Him. Tell Him the things that trouble you. Ask for forgiveness. And ask everything in Jesus' name (from John 14:13).

THE LORD'S PRAYER

CD 2

SONG 19

MY LITTLE PRAYER REMINDER

Before we can pray, "Lord, Thy Kingdom come,"
we must be willing to pray, "My kingdom go."

—Alan Redpath

Thank You, Lord, for Little Things

— A PRAYER ABOUT LITTLE THINGS —

Who says big is better? Little drops of rain fall on little seeds. Little seeds grow into pretty little flowers. Thank God for little things!

Lord, I thank You on this day
For all the little things You've made.
For little drops of rain that fall
On little seeds that grow so tall.
Thank You for the little things,
The little rose that blooms in spring.
Bless little children everywhere,
Keep them in Your love and care.
And may they say with heav'nly delight,
This little prayer we say tonight.

Jesus loved little things too! That's why He said, "Let the *little* children come to me" (Matthew 19:14, emphasis added).

My Little Prayer Reminder

Any concern too small to be turned into a prayer
is too small to be made into a burden.

—Corrie Ten Boom

The Evil One Trembles

The evil one would like nothing more than for Christians to stop praying. Why? He's not afraid of a church that doesn't pray. He's not scared of a family that doesn't pray. They have no power over him. But when we pray, he trembles.

There is no power greater than
A praying woman or praying man.
The evil one trembles, scared is he,
When Christians pray on bended knee.

No fear has he of a prayerless church,
A prayerless man, or prayerless work.
But when we call on God in prayer
He flees, for this he cannot bear.

There is power in prayer—the power of God. God is greater than the devil. So when you pray, that ol' devil trembles and runs away!

My Little Prayer Reminder

No one is a firmer believer in the power of prayer than the devil;

not that he practices it, but he suffers from it.

—Guy H. King

The Prayer of Mary

Mary was a special young woman. She loved the Lord with all her heart. God chose her to be the mother of Jesus. When an angel appeared, telling Mary what would soon happen, Mary prayed:

"My soul glorifies the Lord and my spirit rejoices in God my Savior, for he has been mindful of the humble state of his servant."
—Luke 1:46-48

Mary praised God for all He had planned for her. You are part of God's plan too! You were created by God on purpose, for His purpose! So praise Him!

MY LITTLE PRAYER REMINDER

Our lips sing praise. Our hearts pray it.

A Treasure

Long ago pirates sailed the seven seas. They were looking for treasure. Gold and silver were what they wanted. They spent their lives seeking riches. But there's another kind of treasure. It's more valuable than gold.

Friendship is a treasure,
So rare in many ways.
A friend can make me happy
When together we do play.

But if a friend can't be found,
I need only to recall,
Jesus, You're my best friend,
Who loves me most of all!

Your treasure is what you value and seek after the most. Seek Jesus. He is the greatest treasure—and the greatest friend—of all!

MY LITTLE PRAYER REMINDER

Nothing tends more to cement the hearts of Christians than praying together.

—Charles Finney

Protect and Bless

BY DR. ALBERT SCHWEITZER

Dr. Albert Schweitzer was a missionary. *Missionaries* are people who tell others about God's love. He traveled from his home in Germany all the way to Africa. There he set up a hospital with his wife on the banks of the Ogoouè River. He prayed:

> Oh heavenly Father,
> protect and bless all things that have breath:
> guard them from all evil and let them sleep in peace.

Dr. Schweitzer knew that God loved the African people. He wanted to share God's love by helping them get well. One day, you could be a missionary too!

MY LITTLE PRAYER REMINDER

Prayers can go where people can't.

A Prayer of Jesus

Jesus knew the world was full of two kinds of people: those who trust God and those who do not. So Jesus prayed:

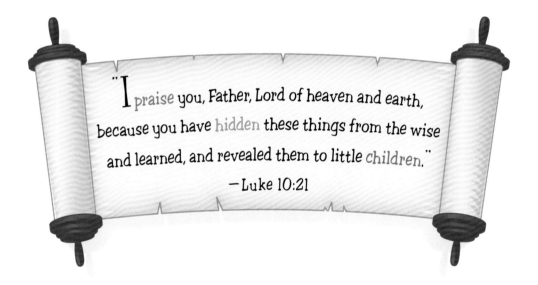

"I praise you, Father, Lord of heaven and earth, because you have hidden these things from the wise and learned, and revealed them to little children."
—Luke 10:21

The "wise and learned" are those who do not trust God. They trust in themselves. But the "children" of God trust Him. Like a little child, they depend on their Father for every need. They talk to Him about every decision. Jesus praises childlike faith. So let's trust Him every day!

MY LITTLE PRAYER REMINDER

You may ask me for anything in my name, and I will do it.

—John 14:14

155

Who Tucks Me In?

God has created a lot of wonderful things. But parents are at the top of the list. They have a way of making everything all right. With one little hug, they can wipe away our biggest tears. They help us forget all our troubles.

Who tucks me in when nights are cold?
Who always has a hand to hold?
Who builds me up when things fall down
And turns my frowny face around?

Who makes it better when I cry?
I think you know, and so do I!
It's Mom and Dad I'm thinking of.
Bless them, Father, with Your love.

The Bible says to honor our father and mother. This means we obey them and thank them for all they do. We pray for them too!

My Little Prayer Reminder

Pray for your parents every day!

Put Down My Toys

What makes a kid happy? That's easy—playtime! What makes God happy? That's easy too—prayer time. Part of growing up is loving God more and our things less.

Lord, as a child this I thought,
"Come see all the toys I've got!"

But as I grew and learned to pray,
You helped me put my toys away.

Now my toys don't mean a thing.
I say, "Come see Christ the King!"

It's okay to enjoy your toys. But don't forget to pray!

MY LITTLE PRAYER REMINDER

It would be much better to forget to play than to forget to pray!

The Prayer of a Tax Collector

A Sinner's Prayer

Jesus once told this story: Two men went to the temple to pray. One was a Pharisee, a leader in the temple. He was very proud. He thanked God that he was better than other people. But the other man was a tax collector. He knew that only God was holy. So he prayed:

"God, have mercy on me, a sinner."

—Luke 18:13

The Pharisee compared himself to other people. But the tax collector compared himself to God. God is our measure of goodness, not other people.

My Little Prayer Reminder

In all your prayers forget not to thank the Lord for his mercies.

—John Bunyan

Dear Father in Heaven

No one knows where heaven is. You can't fly there in a plane or drive there in a car. But heaven is real. It's the place where God lives. He looks down from heaven and watches over you and me. He loves us so much!

Dear Father in heaven,
Look down from above;
Bless Mommy and Daddy
And those whom I love.

May angels watch over
My slumbers, and when
The morning is breaking,
Awake me. Amen.

—Traditional

God watches over you and the people you love too! And from some heavenly window, He listens for someone to say, "Father, I love you."

MY LITTLE PRAYER REMINDER

Pray in the Spirit on all occasions.

—Ephesians 6:18

Thy Love Before, Behind Us

FROM A POEM BY CHRISTINA ROSSETTI

You can't be two places at the same time, can you? No, you can't. But God can! God is here. God is there. God is everywhere. And so is God's love—all at the same time. It's hard to imagine, but it's true!

O Lord, seek us, O Lord, find us
In Thy patient care;
Be Thy love before, behind us
Round us, everywhere.
Turn not from us, call to mind us,
Find, embrace us, bear;
Be Thy love before, behind us,
Round us, everywhere.

Across the ocean, across the desert, or just across the street—no matter where you go, God's love is there for you.

My Little Prayer Reminder

Prayer is the path connecting heaven to earth.

Jesus' Prayer for You

A PRAYER FOR NEW BELIEVERS

Jesus knew that His time on earth was coming to an end. So He prayed for His disciples. He asked His Father to bless and protect them. Jesus wanted them to keep working for Him and never stop. Then Jesus prayed:

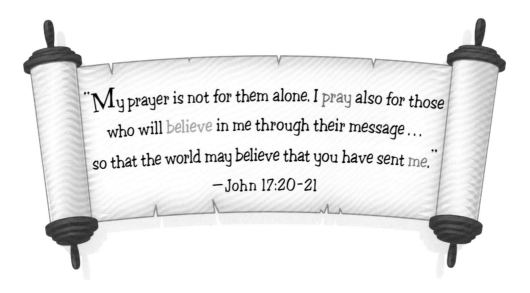

"My prayer is not for them alone. I pray also for those who will believe in me through their message . . . so that the world may believe that you have sent me."
—John 17:20-21

Jesus not only prayed for His disciples, He also prayed for all future believers—that's you and me!

I KNOW THAT MY REDEEMER LIVES • SONG ABOUT JESUS: CD 2 SONG 31

MY LITTLE PRAYER REMINDER

Never say you will pray about a thing; pray about it.

—Oswald Chambers

A Little Traveler's Prayer

Traveling can be lots of fun. We may travel to places across town or places across the ocean. But it's nice to know this one thing: whether we travel near or far, God is always there to greet us when we arrive! There is no place God isn't!

As we travel to and fro'
From here to there each day,
Lord, please before us go
And guide us on the way.
Roads can take us near and far,
But this I know is true,
Lord, no matter where we are,
We're never far from You!

Whether you are traveling forty steps or forty thousand miles, don't worry. God is already waiting there with arms open wide!

MY LITTLE PRAYER REMINDER

I have been driven many times to my knees by the
overwhelming conviction that I had nowhere else to go.

—Abraham Lincoln

from Missa Solemnis

BY LUDWIG VON BEETHOVEN

Beethoven was a great composer who wrote beautiful music. But his prayer was quite simple. He prayed for peace. *Peace* is an easy word to say. But it is very hard to find.

> Lord, grant us peace.

Some people spend a lifetime searching for peace. But Beethoven knew that lasting peace is found in God alone. To find peace, you must find God.

MY LITTLE PRAYER REMINDER

Prayer brings peace in the midst of storm, calm in the face of disaster.

The Apostle's Prayer

PRAY FOR GOD'S GUIDANCE

Judas betrayed Jesus and left. Now there were eleven disciples, not twelve. They needed to choose another disciple to take Judas' place. Led by Peter, the other disciples chose two men. Then they asked God to guide their decision:

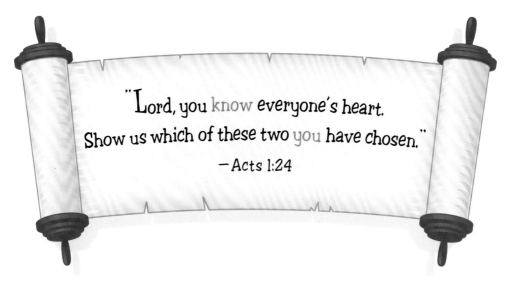

"Lord, you know everyone's heart. Show us which of these two you have chosen."
—Acts 1:24

God helped them choose Matthias. Should we pray when making important decisions? Yes! Always ask God to help you choose what is best.

MY LITTLE PRAYER REMINDER

Prayer is a choice between going with God or going alone.

Teach Me

A PRAYER ABOUT LOVE

There are some things we don't have to learn. No one has to teach us to breathe. We just do it. We don't have to learn to be selfish. We do that very well too. That's why we ask God to teach us His way of doing things.

> Lord, teach me to love,
> Teach me to pray,
> Teach me to walk
> In Your Word each day.
>
> Lord, teach me to be
> Patient and kind.
> Teach me Your way,
> O God of mine.

Jesus came to earth to show us how to live in a way that pleases God. So let's try to live like Jesus!

My Little Prayer Reminder

The greatest tragedy of life is not unanswered prayer, but unoffered prayer.

—F. B. Meyer

Prayer for Trust in Jesus

BY ST. IGNATIUS OF LOYOLA

We can be such worriers, can't we? We worry about the weather. We worry about what friends might say. We even worry about worrying! Yet Jesus taught us to live "worry-free." How? By pointing to some little birds. Birds don't plant or gather, but God feeds them. He'll take care of you too.

O Christ Jesus, when all is darkness
and we feel our weakness and helplessness,
give us the sense of Your presence,
Your love, and Your strength.
Help us to have perfect trust
in Your protecting love
and strengthening power,
so that nothing may frighten or worry us,
for living close to You,
we shall see Your hand,
Your purpose, Your will through all things.

So give your worries some wings . . . and watch them fly away!

LET EVERYTHING THAT HAS BREATH

CD 2
SONG 36

MY LITTLE PRAYER REMINDER

No amount of worry will ever change God's will. Only prayer changes things.

The Prayer of Stephen

The Jewish leaders were angry with Stephen. He would not stop speaking the truth about Jesus. To punish him, they dragged him out of the city, and they stoned him. Poor Stephen! But even as they did this awful thing, Stephen prayed:

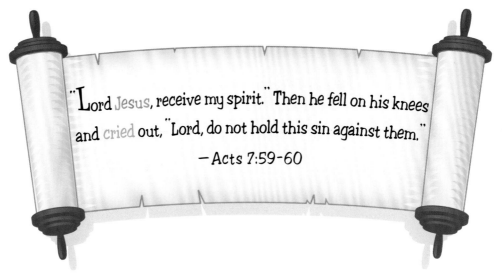

"Lord Jesus, receive my spirit." Then he fell on his knees and cried out, "Lord, do not hold this sin against them."
—Acts 7:59-60

Like Stephen, we must stand up for Jesus. People may be offended, but God is pleased!

MY LITTLE PRAYER REMINDER

I live in the spirit of prayer; I pray as I walk about,
when I lie down, and when I rise up!

—George Müller

Father, God to Thee

When we speak to someone, we call them by name. Prayer is speaking to God. So how should we begin each prayer? By calling God's name. This prayer addresses God the Father:

Father, God to Thee I pray,
Guide and guard me through this day.
As the shepherd tends the lamb
Lord, keep me safe wherever I am.

Keep my feet from every snare,
Keep me with Thy watchful care . . .
And Father when my life is past,
Take me home to heaven at last.
—Traditional

When someone calls your name, you listen. So let each prayer begin by addressing your heavenly Father. He listens too!

MY LITTLE PRAYER REMINDER

The right way to pray is to stretch out our hands and
ask of One who we know has the heart of a Father.

—Dietrich Bonhoeffer

Learning about God

Sir Isaac Newton was one of the most important scientists of all time. Newton discovered the law of gravity. *Gravity* is why we don't float away. Yet, Newton wrote more about the Bible than about science. He believed that God *created* gravity, and that he only discovered it.

Great thinkers cannot craft a bird
Or fashion butterflies;
They can only seek to know
What God has done, and why.

They watch the oceans pound the shore
But they cannot create
A single drop of water.
O God, You are so great!

Science is man's way of discovering what God has already done. Who says that a scientist can't believe in God? Isaac Newton did. Very smart!

MY LITTLE PRAYER REMINDER

Prayer is the gravity that pulls us closer to God.

A Prayer of Paul

Teaching God's Word, day after day, can be tiring. Paul knew this. So he prayed for church leaders. He asked God to give them strength. Not just big muscles on the outside, but big strength on the inside. That kind of strength and power only God can give.

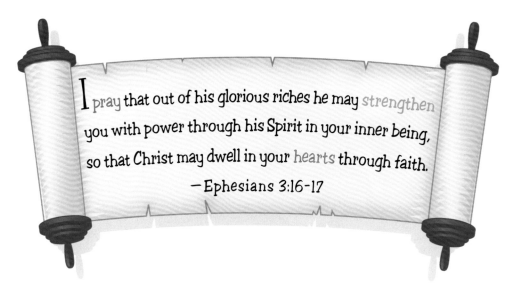

I pray that out of his glorious riches he may strengthen you with power through his Spirit in your inner being, so that Christ may dwell in your hearts through faith.

—Ephesians 3:16-17

Just as a light bulb is powered by electricity, we are powered by God. Pray that God will light up your life!

PAULS SONG: LET THE LIGHT OF JESUS SHINE
CD 2
SONG 40

MY LITTLE PRAYER REMINDER

Heaven is full of answers to prayers for which no one ever bothered to ask.

—Billy Graham

O Blessed Lord, Protect Us

Have you ever wondered why men used to carry shields in battle? Shields protect. They are made of metal. Metal is very strong. It can be struck by a swinging sword, and it will still protect the soldier. God is our shield. He protects us.

O blessed Lord, protect me please
And my dear parents graciously;
Let Your strong arm be ever near
To brothers and to sisters dear.
And all our loved ones in the land,
Shield them with Your own right hand.

—Traditional

God placed us in families. They provide protection and love. So we pray for our family. Prayer is a strong shield too. It covers your family with God's love and protection. That's strong! So pray for your family every day.

MY LITTLE PRAYER REMINDER

Pray often, for prayer is a shield to the soul.

—John Bunyan

Bless My Home

BY JOHN MARTIN

They say "home is where your heart is." That may be true. But a godly home is where the Spirit of God is. And where the Spirit of God is, there is always joy. In a world filled with so much sadness, it's nice to have joy in your home!

God make our home a house of joy,
Where love and peace are given;
It is the dearest place on earth,
The nearest place to heaven.

Invite God to be a part of your family. He always accepts the invitation! And He will fill your house with joy!

My Little Prayer Reminder

He who has learned to pray has learned
the greatest secret of a holy and happy life.

—William Law

Paul's Prayer for Believers

Prayers Can Equip Us

The apostle Paul believed that prayer was powerful. That's why he asked his friends to pray for him. He knew that God would hear. He knew God would supply every need. Paul prayed for other believers too!

May the God of peace . . . equip you
with everything good for doing his will.
— Hebrews 13:20-21

Paul prayed that believers would be "equipped." That means you are ready for anything. Pray and read God's word, and then you will be equipped too!

MY LITTLE PRAYER REMINDER

Praying men . . . do His work and carry out His plans.

—E. M. Bounds

At the Close of Every Day

Sometimes people kneel to pray. They may also bow their heads and put their hands together as a sign of a humble heart. Having a "humble heart" means knowing that God is great and they are not.

At the close of every day,
Lord to You I kneel and pray.
Look upon Your little child,
Look in love and mercy mild.

O forgive and wash away
All my naughtiness this day.
When I sleep and when I wake
Bless me for my Savior's sake.
—Traditional

Whether kneeling or standing, come to God with a humble heart. Say with your body and your heart, "God, You are great."

MY LITTLE PRAYER REMINDER

The men who have done the most for God
in this world have been early on their knees.

—E. M. Bounds

An Eighteenth-Century Grace

BY JOHN CENNICK

Grace is a word we hear a lot at church. Grace means we receive a gift we did not earn. If I received $20 for mowing grass, I earned it. But if I receive $20 for doing nothing, it's a gift . . . it's *grace*! God's grace is better than money. It is love and forgiveness.

Be present at our table, Lord;
Be here and everywhere adored.
Thy creatures bless, and grant that we
May feast in paradise with Thee.

As a reminder of God's grace, we say "grace" before meals. We thank Him for our food, for Jesus, and for all He has done.

My Little Prayer Reminder:

Prayer is a gift we should open every morning.

The Prayer of the Twenty-Four Elders

Jesus is worthy. *Worthy* means "earned the right." When a scout receives a merit badge, he is worthy. He has *earned the right* to receive the award. Jesus is worthy. He *earned the right* to be praised for what He did for us on the cross. That is why the elders in heaven pray:

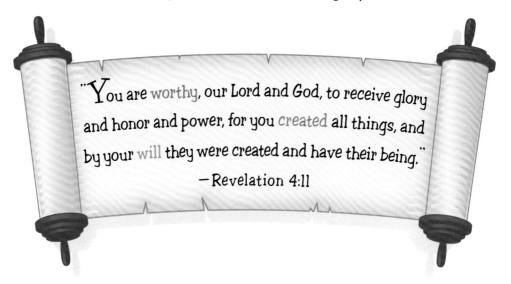

"You are worthy, our Lord and God, to receive glory and honor and power, for you created all things, and by your will they were created and have their being."
—Revelation 4:11

On the cross, Jesus gave us the right to see God and the right to live forever with Him. Jesus is worthy of our praise!

MY LITTLE PRAYER REMINDER

Prayer moves the hand that moves the world.

—John Aikman Wallace

Holy Father

What does Jesus look like? No one has a photograph of Him. But it isn't how Jesus looked that matters anyway. It is how He lived. Jesus always did the right thing at just the right time. We want to live like Jesus—full of love, gentleness, and kindness. So we pray this little prayer:

Holy Father, give us
Each a lowly mind;
Make us more like Jesus,
Gentle, pure, and kind.

Holy Father, help us
Daily by Thy might
What is wrong to conquer
And to choose the right.

—Traditional

We can never be perfect like Jesus. But we can ask God to make us a little more like Jesus every day.

MY LITTLE PRAYER REMINDER

True prayer is measured by weight, and not by length.

—Charles Spurgeon

Lamb of God, I Look to Thee

BY CHARLES WESLEY

A *role model* is someone who sets an example for others. You want to be like your role model. You try to do the things they do. Who, then, of all the people who ever lived should be your role model? If you say Jesus, you are right!

> Lamb of God, I look to Thee;
> Thou shalt my example be;
> Thou art gentle, meek, and mild,
> Thou wast once a little child.
>
> Loving Jesus, gentle Lamb,
> In Thy gracious hands I am;
> Make me Savior, what Thou art,
> Live Thyself within my heart.

Try to do and say the things He taught us to. Then you will begin to look a lot like Jesus!

please help

MY LITTLE PRAYER REMINDER

Prayer is not pulling God to my will,
but the aligning of my will to the will of God.

—E. Stanley Jones

The Prayer of Heaven

THE HALLELUJAH PRAYER

One day all believers will walk the streets of heaven. We will stand before the throne of God. Together, we will sing, "Hallelujah!" That means "praise the name of God." This prayer of praise will echo down every street in heaven:

"Hallelujah! For our Lord God Almighty reigns. Let us rejoice and be glad and give him glory!"
—Revelation 19:6-7

Our God rules over the greatest of all kingdoms. Best of all, through prayer, you can talk to the King Himself. Hallelujah!

MY LITTLE PRAYER REMINDER

Learn to worship God as the God who does wonders.

—Andrew Murray

Gentle Jesus

BY CHARLES WESLEY

Has anyone ever asked you, "Does Jesus live in your heart?" They are asking if you trust Jesus to save you from sin.

Gentle Jesus, meek and mild
Look upon a little child.
Make me gentle as Thou art,
Come and live within my heart.

Take my childish hand in Thine,
Guide these little feet of mine...
And the world shall always see
Christ, the Holy Child, in me!

How can Jesus live in your heart? First, *pray* . . . tell God you are sorry for your sins. Then, *say* . . . tell someone that Jesus now lives in your heart. *Pray* and *say*!

MY LITTLE PRAYER REMINDER

Prayer opens the door to Jesus.

Index of Prayers

Index of Authors